DATE DUE

DATE DUE   ROOM
                                            NUMBER

LET'S LOOK AT RAIN

Jacqueline Dineen

Language consultant
Diana Bentley
University of Reading

Artist
Carolyn Scrace

Let's Look At

Bikes

Castles

Colours

Dinosaurs

Farming

Horses

Outer Space

Rain

Sunshine

Tractors

Trucks

The Seasons

Editor: Rhoda Nottridge

First published in 1988 by
Wayland (Publishers) Ltd
61 Western Road, Hove
East Sussex BN3 1JD, England
© Copyright 1988 Wayland (Publishers) Ltd

British Library Cataloguing in Publication Data
Dineen, Jacqueline
    Let's look at rain.
    1. Rain – For children
    I. Title
    551.57'81

    ISBN 1–85210–218–7

Phototypeset by Kalligraphics Ltd, Redhill, Surrey
Printed and bound by Casterman, S.A., Belgium

Words printed in **bold** are explained in the glossary

Contents

What is rain?

What is rain? It is water that falls from clouds in the sky. Rainwater is called fresh water. It does not taste salty like the water in the sea.

How does the rain get into the sky? It has been raining for millions of years, so there must be a lot up there! Water rises into the sky from the seas, rivers and lakes on earth. Then it falls again as rain. This is going on all the time.

Why we need rain

If it did not rain the whole world would dry up. The sun would dry up the seas, rivers and lakes. Soon the whole earth would be a **desert**.

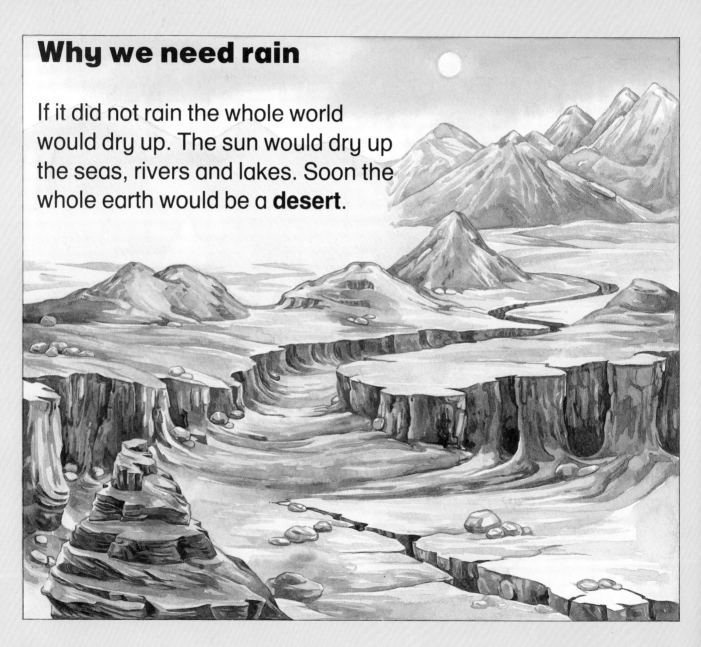

Plants need water to grow. People and animals need water to drink and for cooking and washing. Modern factories need huge amounts of water. It is even used to make electricity. Think of all the ways you use water each day. Can you imagine life without it?

How rain falls

It is difficult to imagine water rising from the earth. How does this happen?

The water in the seas, rivers and lakes is cold.

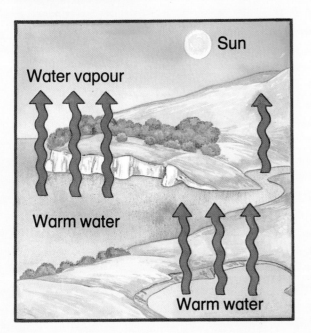

The sun shines and warms some of it up. The warm water turns into steam, or water **vapour**. Warm air always rises. The water vapour rises up into the sky with the warm air.

Then it meets cold air and is cooled down.

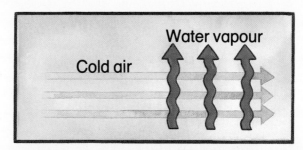

This turns the water vapour back into drops of water.

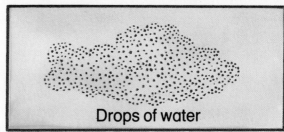

The drops mass together and form clouds. When the clouds become heavy, the drops fall to the earth as rain.

What happens to the rain?

The rain falls into the seas, rivers and lakes and on to the land.

Land is made up of hard rocks, soft rocks and soil. Some rain seeps through soft rocks and soil until it comes to a layer of hard rock. It cannot soak through the hard rock so some of it collects underground.

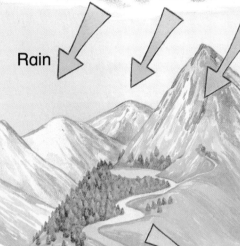

Cloud

Rain

River water

Soil
Soft rock
Water
Hard rock

When it rains, most water flows downhill towards the sea.
   The sun shines on the fallen rain. It changes it into water vapour again. And so the cycle goes on.

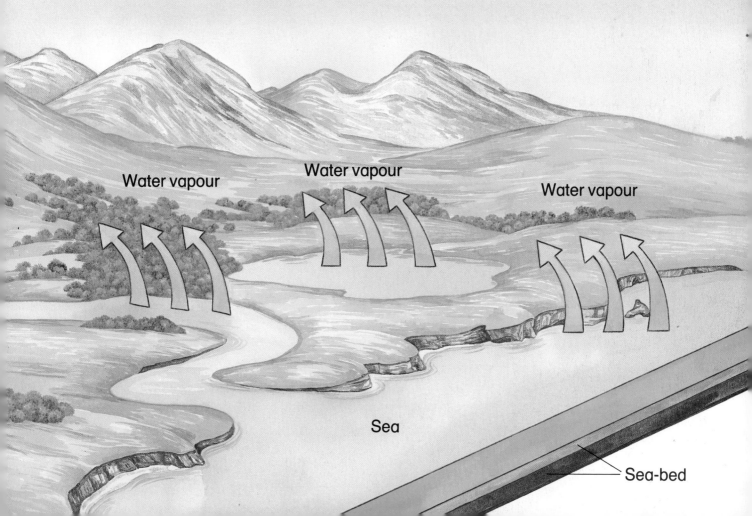

Sun

Water vapour

Water vapour

Water vapour

Sea

Sea-bed

Frozen rain

Sometimes the water vapour rises up very high in the sky. The air is so cold that the water drops freeze. They fall to the earth as snow or hail.

There is always snow on the ground in very cold countries. Some countries have a cold season, when it snows only in winter.

12

Hail sometimes falls during summer thunderstorms. The frozen drops are thrown high in the air by the storm. They grow bigger as more water freezes round them. The hailstones melt when they touch the ground.

13

Rain clouds

Clouds do not always bring rain.
Look at the picture. The very high
wispy clouds are drops of ice. The
other thin, high clouds bring good
weather. The striped clouds in the
middle layer mean light rain. The
puffy clouds in the middle show that
it could rain if they pile up.

Good weather

Rain and storms

14

Ice

Light rain

Rain

Low clouds often bring bad
weather. The dark masses of cloud
mean rain or storms. The low, dark
sheets bring heavy rain or snow. It
may rain if there is low cloud, such
as fog.

Fog and rain

15

Where rain falls

A lot of rain falls near coasts. Water vapour rises from the sea. Winds blow it across the land. The heat from the land makes the vapour rise and turn into rain clouds.

Rain

Wind

Rain cloud

Water vapour

Wind

Hot air

Sometimes the winds blow water vapour on to a mountainside. It is forced to rise higher and turns into rain.

Different parts of the world have different **climates**. In some places it rains evenly all the year round. In some hot places, it rains every day. The plants that live here can become enormous.

In other hot places, it hardly ever rains. Very few plants can live in these areas.

Too much rain

Windmill

Sometimes it rains too much. Rivers fill up and burst their banks. The land is **flooded**.

   Holland is a very flat country. In many parts of Holland the land and the sea are at the same level. This means water from the sea and rivers can easily flood the land. To stop this the people in Holland have built strong walls called **dykes** to hold back flood water. Windmills pump water away from the land. It is carried away in **canals**.

Dyke

Canal

Dyke

Sudden floods do a lot of harm.
Homes and **crops** are ruined.

19

The rainy season

What is a 'rainy season'? It happens in parts of Africa and Asia where it is dry for months. Then it rains for months. These countries have a rainy season.

Rainy season

Desert

Other

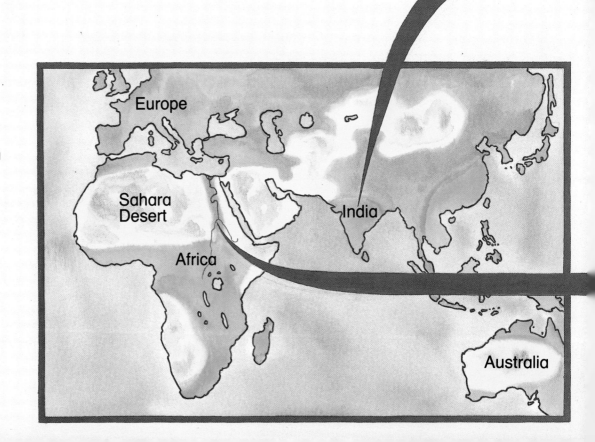

Farmers make use of the rains. Rice grows in flooded fields. It is an important crop in many parts of Asia.

Egypt is very dry. The River Nile is the only river. It starts in a part of Africa where there is a rainy season. People settled by the River Nile 6,000 years ago. The river flooded every summer. The people grew crops in the soaked earth.

Monsoons

India and Pakistan have a rainy season. It is brought by the **monsoon** winds. In summer, warm wet winds blow in from the Indian Ocean. The warm air rises over the land. Heavy rains fall. When this happens it is called the monsoon time. Houses near rivers are built on high ground or on **stilts** because of floods that happen during the monsoons.

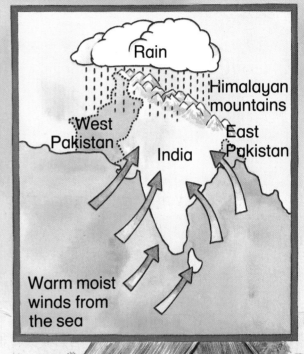

Rain

Himalayan mountains

West Pakistan

East Pakistan

India

Warm moist winds from the sea

In winter, cool dry winds blow from the land to the sea. The weather is dry.

The farmers plant rice in the wet season. Some farmers grow wheat in the dry season. Some people can grow only a few crops for their families. Farming is hard when the land is too dry or too wet.

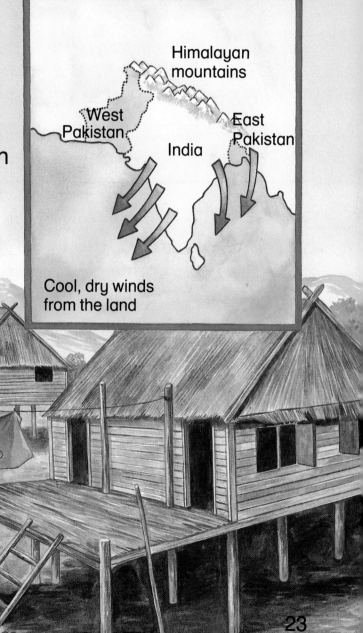

Himalayan mountains

West Pakistan

East Pakistan

India

Cool, dry winds from the land

23

Too little rain

It hardly ever rains in the desert. Plants cannot grow there. The picture shows an **oasis** in the desert. Underground water has come to the surface and formed a pool. Plants can grow near the water. People settle here. They grow crops such as date palms.

If it does not rain for a long time, there is a **drought**. People are told not to use too much water.

In countries with one rainy season a year, a drought is very serious. The land dries up. Crops will not grow. People and animals starve unless food is brought in from other countries.

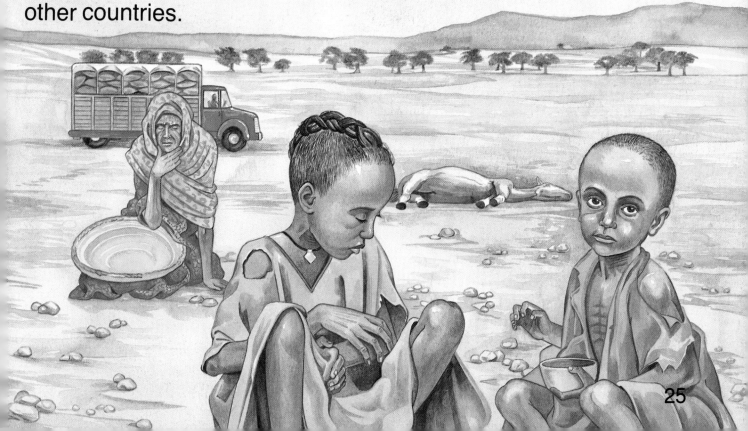

25

Storing rain

We need fresh water all the year round. We have to store rainwater. If we did not, it would seep into the ground or flow into the sea.

Water is stored in large lakes called **reservoirs**. A river flows in at one end and there is a **dam** at the other end. This keeps the water in.

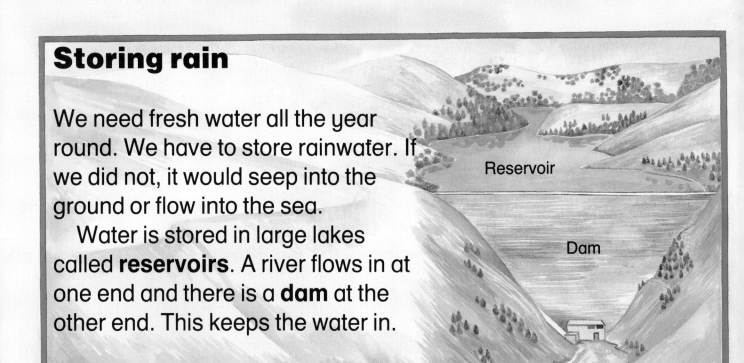

Reservoir

Dam

Some of it is used to water farmland. We call this **irrigation**.

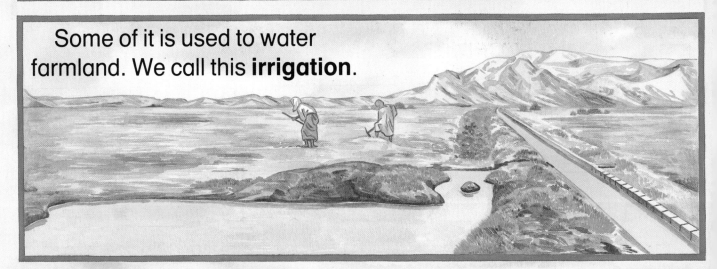

Some is taken to people's homes.

We use underground water, too. People dig wells to reach it. Some people study the land to find new supplies of underground water. They are called **hydrologists**. If they find water it is piped to the surface and stored in reservoirs.

Drilling to find water

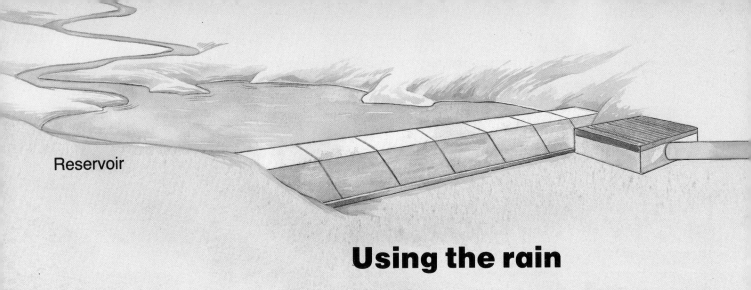
Reservoir

Using the rain

Water has to be cleaned before we can drink it. It is pumped from the reservoir to a waterworks. Here, it is cleaned so that people can drink it. Then it is pumped into storage tanks.

Offices

Houses

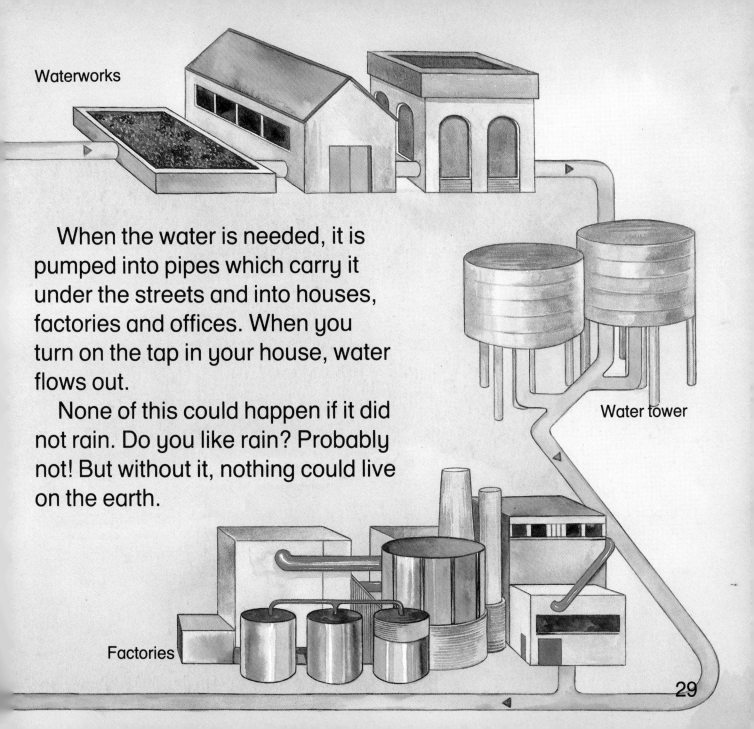

Waterworks

When the water is needed, it is pumped into pipes which carry it under the streets and into houses, factories and offices. When you turn on the tap in your house, water flows out.

None of this could happen if it did not rain. Do you like rain? Probably not! But without it, nothing could live on the earth.

Water tower

Factories

Glossary

Canal   A water channel for draining the land.

Climate   The usual type of weather in a country.

Crops   Plants that are grown for food.

Dam   A strong concrete wall that holds back a river so that a lake forms behind it.

Desert   A hot dry area of land where the soil is sandy and there are no plants.

Drought   A long time without rain.

Dyke   A long wall that holds back flood water.

Flooded   Covered with water.

Hydrologist   Someone who studies the land and the rocks under the surface to find underground water.

Irrigation   To water land by digging ditches from a river or lake to the fields.

Monsoon   A wind in Asia that brings a rainy season.

Oasis   A place in the desert where underground water rises to the surface.

Reservoir   A lake that builds up behind a dam and is used for storing water.

Stilts   Long poles that raise a building off the ground.

Vapour   A cloud made of very tiny liquid drops, such as steam from a kettle.

Books to read

Rivers, Valerie Pitt (Franklin
    Watts, 1978)
Rivers and River Life,
Macdonald
    First Library (Macdonald
    Educational Books, 1971)
Snow, Macdonald Starters
    (Macdonald Educational
    Books, 1971)
Snow and Ice, Philip
    Sauvain (Franklin Watts,
    1978)
Water, P.J. Hunt (Franklin
    Watts, 1977)

Index